Routes to Writing

POETRY

YEAR 2

Author: Elspeth Graham
Series Editor: Amanda George
Series Advisers: Monica Hughes *and* Isabel MacDonald

Contents

OXFORD
UNIVERSITY PRESS

Unit Objective: *To use poems as a model for writing*

About the Poems in this Unit

Purpose	For entertainment and enjoyment. To express meaning through choice of words, word patterns, rhyme and rhythm.		
Poems in this Unit			
	Shared Writing: *My Home*	**Guided Writing Easier Text** *Chips and Ice Cream: Red* (page 5) *Recipe for a Saturday Morning* (page 8)	**Guided Writing Harder Text** *Dinosaur Dreams: Motorway, Motorway* (page 13) *The Family Wash* (page 7)
Type of Poem			
	My Home – poem with familiar setting, using flexible rhythm and rhyme scheme	*Red* – list poem with familiar setting *Recipe* – recipe poem with familiar setting	*Motorway* – poem with patterned language and familiar setting *The Family Wash* – shape poem with familiar setting
Organisation			
Verses	Four verses	*Red* four verses *Recipe* not divided into verses	*Motorway* two verses, two refrains *The Family Wash* not divided into verses
Language Features			
Rhythm	Uses flexible rhythm with some differences between verses	*Red* no rhythm *Recipe* no rhythm	*Motorway* strong, regular rhythm *The Family Wash* strong, regular rhythm
Rhyme	Uses rhyme throughout, both within lines and at ends of lines	*Red* no rhyme *Recipe* no rhyme	*Motorway* uses rhyme in refrain *The Family Wash* regular rhyme scheme
Use of patterns/ repetition	All four verses have a different pattern. Some phrases are repeated.	*Red* each verse starts with same four words *Recipe* pattern/ repetition comes from recipe format	*Motorway* strong pattern and repetition *The Family Wash* no pattern/repetiton
May not be written in full sentences	Written in full sentences	*Red* written in full sentences *Recipe* no sentences	*Motorway* not written in full sentences *The Family Wash* no sentences

Outline of the Teaching Sessions

Session	Text	Focus	Outcome
Pre-writing and Stimulus Ideas	*My Home*	Identify the main features of the poem	Shared reading: gain familiarity with *My Home* and the concepts of alliteration and rhyme
Shared Writing 1	*My Home*	Identify the subject matter of the poem and use it as a basis for writing	Shared writing: compose sentences in the style of the last two lines of the poem
Shared Writing 2	*My Home*	Identify alliteration in the poem	Shared writing: compose alliterative sentences
Shared Writing 3	*My Home*	Identify the structure and features of the poem	Shared writing: write a new verse
Guided Writing 1 (easier text)	*Chips and Ice Cream: Red*	Identify the structure and meaning of the poem	Guided writing: write another poem based on *Red*
Guided Writing 2 (easier text)	*Chips and Ice Cream: Recipe for a Saturday Morning*	Identify the structure and meaning of the poem	Guided writing: write a new version of the poem
Guided Writing 1 (harder text)	*Dinosaur Dreams: Motorway, Motorway*	Identify the structure and meaning of the poem	Guided writing: write a new poem with a similar structure
Guided Writing 2 (harder text)	*Dinosaur Dreams: The Family Wash*	Identify the structure of the poem	Guided writing: write a new version of the poem
Independent Writing	Generic (PCM 5)	Understand the features of a shape poem	Independent writing: write a snail shape poem
	Generic (PCM 6)	Read and comment on poems by different poets	Independent writing: fill in chart with poem titles and opinions
	Big Book: *The World of Weird* (PCM 7)	Understand the features of a nonsense poem	Independent writing: own version of nonsense poem

Planning

Routes to Writing is a very flexible programme. We have provided a suggested route through the different elements of the unit (please see below). However, you may decide on a different route depending on the ability levels of the children in your class. For example, if the children are confident and able writers, they may require less teacher modelling before they 'have a go' for themselves. Whilst we would strongly recommend that you follow the progression of shared writing leading to guided writing leading to independent writing, the way in which you choose to use the programme can be adapted to suit the needs of your children.

	Shared Writing	Guided Writing	Independent Writing	Plenary
Monday	Pre-writing and Stimulus Ideas – share Big Book			
Tuesday	Pre-writing and Stimulus Ideas	Guided Writing Session 1 (easier text)	Independent Writing	Session Plenary
Wednesday	Shared Writing Session 1	Guided Writing Session 1 (harder text)	Independent Writing	Session Plenary
Thursday	Shared Writing Session 2	Guided Writing Session 2 (easier text)	Independent Writing	Session Plenary
Friday	Shared Writing Session 3	Guided Writing Session 2 (harder text)	Independent Writing	Session Plenary

This book gives detailed guidance on shared and guided writing sessions to fit the NLS requirements for Year 2 Term 1. You will also find on pages 7, 12, 13, 14 and 15 suggestions for further sessions that will suit the requirements for Terms 2 and 3.

Curriculum Correlations and Levelling

Curriculum Objectives

Text level objectives covered in this unit

Year 2 Term 1

T7 to learn, reread and recite favourite poems, taking account of punctuation; to comment on aspects such as word combinations, sound patterns and forms of presentation

T12 to use simple poetry structures and to substitute own ideas, write new lines

Year 2 Term 2

T8 to read own poems aloud

T9 to identify and discuss patterns of rhythm, rhyme and other features of sound in different poems

T15 to use structures from poems as a basis for writing; to write own poems from initial jottings and words

Year 2 Term 3

T8 to discuss meanings of words and phrases that create humour and sound effects in poetry, e.g. nonsense poems, tongue-twisters, riddles, and to classify poems into simple types; to make class anthologies

T11 to use humorous verse as a structure for children to write their own by adaptation, mimicry or substitution; select words with care, rereading and listening to their effect

Levelling

Title	ORT level	Average number of words per page	Features that affect level of difficulty
Chips and Ice Cream	6	36	Poems vary in readability, but the collection includes simple rhymes that are easy to read. Hardest words: *shrieked, programmes, mushrooms, breadfruit.*
Dinosaur Dream	7	52	High average word count, but most poems have rhyme which makes them more predictable. Hardest poem is *Dinosaur Dream Recipe* with *prehistoric, quality, landscape, imagination.*

Links to English 5–14 (National Guidelines for Scotland)

Text type	Titles	Level	Attainment targets/programme of study
Poetry	*My Home* *Chips and Ice Cream* *Dinosaur Dream*	B	Imaginative writing: poetry writing depends on wide experience of listening to and reading poems with discussion of structures and effects. At this stage content, rhythm and vocabulary are more important than rhyme.

Using the Shared and Guided Writing Poems Throughout Year 2

This book gives you full notes for using a selection of poems which are just right for Year 2 Term 1. The featured poems match the NLS requirements for that term particularly closely. However, the Big Book and the Pupil Book contain a wealth of poems which are ideal for use in other terms, and brief notes are given to help you use some of these poems too.

The *Poetry Pupil Book* is divided into two mini-anthologies, one at an easier and one at a harder level. Each mini-anthology contains poems which match *all* the NLS termly requirements for Year 2. In addition, you'll find each mini-anthology has examples of the same types of poem – such as tongue-twisters, riddles, list poems and recipe poems, etc. This means that all your ability groups can work on poems of the same type, if you wish.

Pre-writing and Stimulus Ideas

Core Language, Context and Concepts

Before using the shared writing sessions, make sure children are familiar with the Big Book poems and some basic features of poetry, including the following:

- rhyming words and alliteration
- rhythm.

Shared Reading

My Home

- This poem with a familiar setting fits well with the NLS range requirements for Year 2 Term 1, though it's also appropriate for use at other times.
- Read the whole poem aloud to the children.
- Read out the first verse in a snake voice, hissing all the *s* sounds. Ask: "Does it sound like the voice of a snake? Why?" Explain that writers sometimes choose words that begin with the same letter, such as 'said', 'snake', 'soft', to get a special effect (alliteration). In this poem the poet has also chosen several other words, like 'this', 'miss', 'hiss', that have the same letter elsewhere in the word (consonance).
- Read out the first verse again. This time ask the children to tell you which words rhyme. Point out that the rhyming words are not just at the ends of the lines – for example, 'sand' and 'land'.
- Read through the second verse. Say: "This verse sounds quite different from the first verse, and looks different on the page." Ask the children to listen for the rhymes – again, not just at the ends of lines. Can the children find any alliteration in this verse?
- Continue in the same way with the rest of the poem. Point out that the first two lines of each verse are similar, although the verses are quite different otherwise.
- Read the whole poem through, and encourage the children to read with you.
- Did the children enjoy the poem? Which verse did they like best?

Other Stimulus Activities

Ten Pin Bowling (Big Book page 17)

- This lively oral poem with predictable and patterned language is a good fit with the NLS range requirements for Year 2 Term 2, and will enable you to focus on inventing new rhyming couplets to add to the poem.
- Read the poem through aloud, and then read it again stressing the rhyme and the rhythm. Point out the repeating lines, "Knock them down . . .", which act as a chorus or refrain.
- Ask: "Has anyone here been bowling?" If so, ask the children to share their experiences to help the class think up some new ideas to add to the poem. For example, how does it feel if you miss the skittles? How does it feel if you hit them?
- Talk about the children's ideas, and write a list of rhyming words to help them write some new rhyming couplets. For example, "miss, this, hiss, kiss," and "hit, fit, kit, it, bit".

The World of Weird (Big Book page 12)

- This funny nonsense poem has plenty of language play, and fits well with the NLS range requirements for Year 2 Term 3. It will enable you to focus on using the structure of the poem as a basis for an additional verse.
- Read the title, and ask: "What do you think the poem will be about?" Read the poem aloud, and encourage the children to join in.
- Explain that this is a nonsense poem, and it's meant to be silly. Encourage the children to have fun by changing words or phrases to make the poem even sillier.
- Ask the children to write a list of ideas for other strange things they might find in the World of Weird – including invented words if they wish.
- Use some of the ideas in a new verse for the poem. Children could follow the session by completing PCM 7 (page 24).

Other Poetry Anthologies

It will be helpful if the children have shared a range of poems in literary sessions. Many good collections and anthologies of poetry are available, including the following:

The King's Pyjamas, edited by Pie Corbett (Belitha Press)
The Way to the Zoo, edited by David Jackson (Oxford University Press)
Once Upon a Rhyme, edited by Sara Corrin (Faber Children's Books)

My Home

"This is my home," said Snake,
with a soft hiss.

"This is what I would miss.
To slide through the scrub
And the dry yellow grass,
Over sand
And land the colour of brass,
Baked by the sun's kiss."

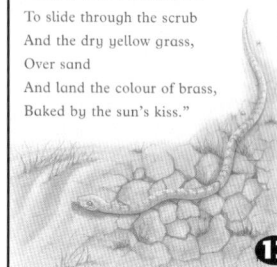

13

Session 1

Focus
Identify the subject matter of the poem and use it as a basis for writing

Outcome
Write sentences in the style of the last two lines of the poem

You will need
- Big Book pages 13–16 or CD-ROM
- Small whiteboards for the children

This session focuses on *My Home*, which is ideal for use in Year 2 Term 1. For shared writing ideas for Year 2 Terms 2 and 3, see page 7.

Talk for Writing

- Read through *My Home*. Ask the children to listen carefully and reread the last verse.
- The last verse is about a girl. Ask the children: "What is she describing?" Point out if necessary that the middle four lines of the verse are about playing in the garden with friends. The last two lines describe the warm and cosy feeling of bedtime.
- Ask: "What would you miss most about your home if you had to leave it?" Give the children a couple of minutes to discuss this, and then jot down some of their suggestions on the board or flipchart.

Teacher Demonstration

- Explain to the children that you're going to write a sentence based on the last two lines of the poem, about some things that are special about your home.
- Think aloud as you write notes, such as: "Snuggling up on the sofa with my dog"; "sharing a pot of tea with my family"; "the big tree in my garden".
- Take one or two of your ideas and write them in a sentence beginning: "This is what I would miss –". See page 11 for an example. Reread and refine your sentence.

Teacher Scribe

- Invite the children to give you a similar sentence about something special to do with their home.
- Choose a few sentences and help the children to refine them if necessary. Say the sentences aloud once or twice before writing them.

Supported Composition

- Ask the children to write on their small whiteboards a list of the things that they would miss most about their homes.
- Ask some of the children to use these ideas to write short sentences beginning: "This is what I would miss –" on the board.

Plenary
Reread the last verse of the poem, and then read some of the new lines you have written. Ask: "Would these lines make a good end to the poem? Why, or why not?"

My Home

"This is my home," said Gull,
with a high cry.

"On this cliff
where stiff winds
lift me sky high,
and the green sea sings below me,
and I drift on spread wings
under the blue sky."

"This is my home," said Bear,
with a sure snore.

"I let winter pass –
when ice is like glass,
and bitter winds blow.
I dig deep with my paws
and long sharp claws
and make a cave in the snow."

"This is my home,"
said Girl, with
a loud shout.

"With friends in my class
I play ball by the wall,
or race round on the grass
while long sunny days pass.

This is what I would miss –
my Ted, my soft bed, and a kiss."

14 **15** **16**

Focus
Identify alliteration in the poem
Outcome
Write alliterative sentences
You will need
- Big Book pages 13–16 or CD-ROM
- Small whiteboards for the children

Session 2

This session focuses on *My Home*, which is ideal for use in Year 2 Term 1. For shared writing ideas for Year 2 Terms 2 and 3, see page 7.

Talk for Writing

- Read the first verse through using your best snakey voice. Read again encouraging the children to join in.
- Remind the children that the poet is using *alliteration*, with all those 's' sounds at the beginning of words, to get a special effect like a snake's hissing. (He is also using *consonance*, with 's' sounds elsewhere in the words.)

Teacher Demonstration

- Tell the children that you're going to write some sentences using alliteration.
- Use the words in the poem to make short alliterative sentences. See page 11 for an example.

Teacher Scribe

- Ask the children to think of words beginning with 'sl'. List the words that they think of, such as 'slide', 'slither', 'slow', 'slimey', 'sly'. Encourage the children to help you sound out and spell the words.
- With the children's help, make another list of words beginning with 'sh' and 'sn'.

Supported Composition

- Ask the children to think of some alliterative sentences using some of the words in your lists. They can write their sentences on small whiteboards if available.
- Choose a child's sentence, say it aloud and refine it if necessary, before writing it on the board – for example, "The silver snake slowly slid and slithered on the sand".
- Ask the children to work in pairs to make lists of words beginning with different letter blends, such as 'sn', 'bl', 'ch'. Can they make some short alliterative sentences with their word lists?

Plenary
Ask the children to read out their sentences. Have they made up full sentences? Are the sentences alliterative? Do they make sense?

Focus
Identify the structure and features of the poem

Outcome
Write a new verse

You will need
- Big Book pages 13–16 or CD-ROM

Session 3

This session focuses on *My Home*, which is ideal for use in Year 2 Term 1. For shared writing ideas for Year 2 Terms 2 and 3, see page 7.

Talk for Writing

- Read through *My Home,* encouraging the children to read with you.
- Discuss the structure of the poem. Ask: "How does each verse begin? What is each verse about?"
- Explain to the children that although each verse is similar they all have slightly different rhythms and rhyme schemes. Clap out the main stresses in each verse (most lines have either two or three main stresses, but the number varies from line to line in each verse). Note where the rhyming words come.

Teacher Demonstration

- Explain to the children that you're going to plan how to write a new verse. Choose an animal to write about, such as a frog. Tell the children that the first thing you're going to do is make a list about what a frog's home might be like.
- Write a list of the kind of places a frog likes and the kind of things a frog likes to do. Write from a frog's point of view, in the first person. Say your ideas out loud before you write them down. See page 11 for an example.

Teacher Scribe

- Ask the children for ideas to start the verse. Say: "Look at *My Home*: how does each verse begin?" Refine the ideas into an opening pair of lines, like: "'This is my home' said Frog,/ with a low croak." Write the lines on the board.
- Ask the children for their ideas for the next lines. They can use your list or ideas of their own. Look for opportunities to use rhymes in the middle or at the end of lines. If it's possible to use alliteration too, so much the better, but keep it fun! Make your verse as long as you like.
- Repeat with other animals if you have time.

Plenary
Read the verse out loud. Does it work? Does it fit with the other verses of the poem? Does it make sense? Does it rhyme?

Shared Writing Examples

Shared Writing Session 1

This is what I would miss —
being cosy and warm on the sofa
when it's raining outside.

Shared Writing Session 2

"Shh," said Snake softly. Snake slid in the scrub.

Shared Writing Session 3

I live in a bog,
I play by a log.
I jump up high,
I leap to and fro.
I love the rain,
I love the fog,
I splish-splash in the water.

"This is my home," said Frog,
with a low croak.

"I love to swim in my bog.
I jump off my log for a joke.
When there is rain or fog,
I love to leap to and fro.
I splish-splash wherever I go."

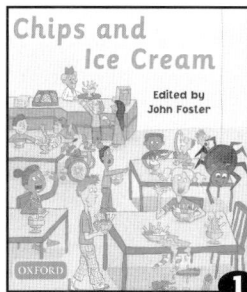

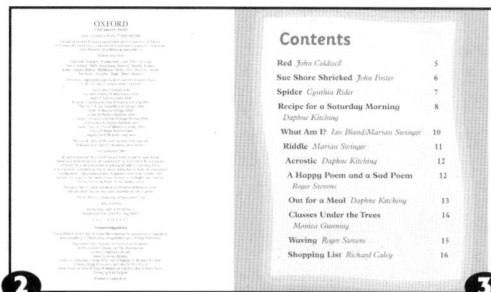

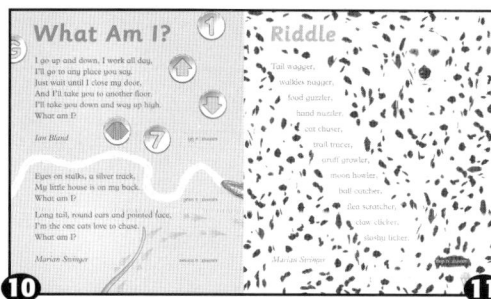

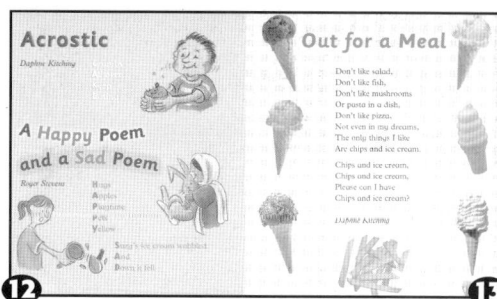

Contents

Focus
Identify the structure and meaning of the poem

Outcome
Write another poem based on *Red*

You will need
- Poetry Pupil Book, *Chips and Ice Cream*, page 5
- PCM 1, page 18

Plenary
Ask the children to read their poems out to the rest of the group. Discuss the ideas that have been used. You could also read Richard Caley's poem *Blue*, on page 5 of *Dinosaur Dream*.

Session 1 *Red*

This session focuses on *Red*, a list poem with a familiar setting which is ideal for use in Year 2 Term 1. For guided writing ideas for Term 2, see the brief notes below. For ideas for Term 3, see the brief notes on page 13.

Talk for Writing
- Read *Red* aloud. Explain that this poem is a collection of feelings about the colour red. Discuss with the children what each verse means. For example, in the first verse, red is about being out of breath (or the feeling of winning a race). In the second verse, red is about embarrassment; in the third verse it is about being hot; and in the last verse it is about danger. Ask: "What does the colour red mean to you?" Share ideas.
- Look at the structure of the poem. It is made up of four verses without rhymes, each with the same beginning. Ask: "What is different about the last verse?" Why do the children think the poet moved the word 'of' up to the first line?

Guided Writing
- Tell the children that they are going to write a poem about the colour blue. Ask them to think about what the colour blue means to them. Encourage them to note all their ideas, such as the sky, Mum's eyes, Dad's car, cold, being sad.
- Give the children PCM 1 and ask them to use some of their ideas to write a poem on the same pattern as *Red*. Support them by talking about the first verse as they write.

Additional Guided Writing Session for Term 2
Out for a Meal (page 13)
- This poem with patterned and predictable language is ideal for Term 2.
- Read the poem and ask the children to help you clap the rhythm. Ask them to spot the rhyming words.
- Ask the children to make notes of some of the foods they particularly like and dislike. They can use these to write their own version of *Out for a Meal*. Write the first few lines as a group.

Focus
Identify the structure and meaning of the poem

Outcome
Write a new version of the poem

You will need
- Poetry Pupil Book, *Chips and Ice Cream*, page 8
- PCM 2, page 19

Plenary
Ask the children to read their poems aloud. Do their poems mention lots of different ingredients? Do they describe the perfect time of day effectively?

Session 2 *Recipe for a Saturday Morning*

This session focuses on *Recipe for a Saturday Morning*, a recipe poem with a familiar setting which is ideal for use in Year 2 Term 1. For guided writing ideas for Term 2, see the brief notes on page 12. For ideas for Term 3, see the brief notes below.

Talk for Writing
- Read through the poem together. Can the children tell you what it is about? The poem describes a 'recipe' for a perfect Saturday morning. Do the children agree that this sounds like a great Saturday morning? Would they prefer anything different?
- Look at the aspects of the poem that are a bit like a recipe – for example, the heading 'Ingredients', the use of numerals instead of number words, the lack of full sentences.

Guided Writing
- Explain to the children that they are going to write their own recipe poem. They can write about their own perfect Saturday morning, or another time of day such as Saturday evening, Sunday bedtime, or Monday morning. Share some ideas before the children write. It may be easiest in terms of preparation if everyone writes about the same time of day.
- Give the children PCM 2 and support them as they write. Remind them to keep to the format of an ingredients list, with numbers and quantities of things, just as the original poem does.

Additional Guided Writing Session for Term 3
Riddle (page 11)
- This riddle in the form of a kenning, using language play, fits well in Term 3.
- Read through the poem and make sure the children understand that it is about a dog. Talk about some of the images and what they mean.
- As a group, write down some phrases to describe a cat. Turn some of them into two-word phrases like those in Riddle, such as "fur licker, bird chaser, cream guzzler, loud purrer . . .".
- Ask them to turn their cat phrases into a poem like *Riddle*.

1

2

Contents

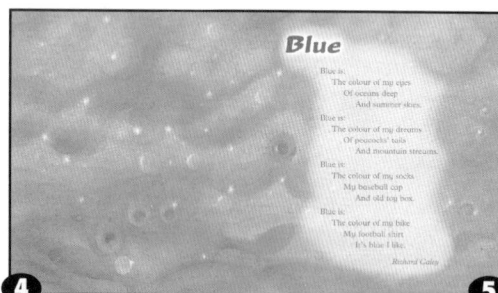

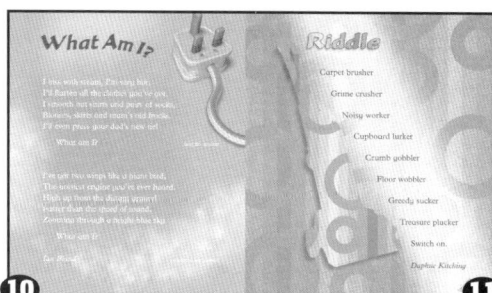

3

4

Blue

5

10

11

12

13

Focus
Identify the structure and meaning of the poem

Outcome
Write a new poem with a similar structure

You will need
● Poetry Pupil Book, *Dinosaur Dreams*, page 13
● PCM 3, page 16

Plenary
Ask the children to share their poems with the rest of the group. Do the poems make sense? Do they describe what it's like being at the seaside?

Session 1 *Motorway, Motorway*

This session focuses on *Motorway, Motorway*, a poem with a familiar setting and patterned language which is ideal for use in Year 2 Term 1. For guided writing ideas for Term 2, see the brief notes below. For ideas for Term 3, see the brief notes on page 15.

Talk for Writing
● Read the poem. Ask: "Who 'sits watching'?" Do the children think that the watchers might be children sitting in the back of a car? Ask: "Have you ever been in a car on a motorway? What was it like?"
● Ask the children to read the poem again and look at its structure. Read the refrain, stressing the strong rhythm and the repeating 'way'. The verses are very similar – only the descriptive words change. Some of these words, like 'zooming' and 'zipping', actually sound like the things they describe (*onomatopoeia*).

Guided Writing
● Explain to the children that they're going to write a poem with a structure like *Motorway, Motorway*. But their poem is going to be about the seaside. Say: "Imagine you're sitting at the seaside. Write a list of people, animals and things that might pass by if you sat at the seaside and watched."
● When they have a few things listed, ask them to write their own version of the poem using PCM 3. Support them as they work.

Additional Guided Writing Session for Term 2
Hopscotch (page 5)
● This is a poem from another culture (Jamaica). It has patterned and predictable language, and is ideal for Term 2.
● Read the poem, then reread it and focus on the rhythm. Clap out the rhythm, particularly in the first verse, and ask the children to join in. Ask them to spot the repeating phrases and the parts of the poem that are particularly fun to say.
● As a group, make up a new first verse (based on the one in *Hopscotch*) about another playground game.

Focus
Identify the structure of the poem

Outcome
Write a new version of the poem

You will need
- Poetry Pupil Book, *Dinosaur Dreams*, page 7
- PCM 4, page 21

Session 2 *The Family Wash*

This session focuses on *The Family Wash*, a shape poem with a familiar setting which is ideal for use in Year 2 Term 1. For guided writing ideas for Term 2, see the brief notes on page 12. For ideas for Term 3, see the brief notes below.

Talk for Writing
- Look at the poem before reading it. Ask: "Why has the poet written the words inside the pictures?" Talk about the way the pictures help the reader understand the poem.
- Read the poem, and ask the children to look out for rhyming words. Point out that the poem is actually a simple rhyme, presented on the page in an interesting way.

Guided Writing
- Explain to the children that they're going to write a similar poem. Give them copies of PCM 4, and tell them that they can write about clothes belonging to different members of their family, or their own favourite clothes hanging on the line. They will need to plan the poem, so ask them to make notes on another sheet of paper. Support them as they do this.
- Children can then turn their notes into lines for the poem. Don't worry about rhyming at this stage. Support them while they draw clothing shapes on PCM 4, and write their lines in.

Additional Guided Writing Session for Term 3
Don't Tell Tales (page 11)
- This is an acrostic poem, which fits well in Term 3.
- Read through the poem with the children. Do they notice anything interesting about it? Point out the initial letters of the lines if necessary, and explain that this type of poem is called an acrostic.
- Read the poem again, and clap out the rhythm of the lines. Point out that all the lines have three main beats, though the number of syllables is not the same in each line.
- Give the children a title for their own acrostic poem, such as *What's For Dinner?* Talk through ideas before they write. Encourage them to keep a constant rhythm, but don't worry about rhyme.

Plenary
Ask the children to swap sheets and read each other's poems. Have they used shapes to help the reader understand the poem?

These activities can be used for group or independent work during the literacy hour.

- Give the children opportunities to read the other poems in the mini-anthologies. Ask them to pick their favourite, and write their own poem in a similar style. Less able writers might benefit from working in small groups or with adult support.

- After reading the acrostic poems on page 12 of *Chips and Ice Cream* or page 12 of *Dinosaur Dreams*, ask the children to write acrostic poems about food. Suggest some ideas, such as BANANAS, NOODLES, CHIPS etc. Collect the poems into a class anthology or use them to make a display.

- Using PCM 5 (page 22) the children could make a snail shape poem. Ask them to write a bank of snaily words in the box at the top of the page. When the children have a bank of words and some good ideas they could set about filling in the snail shape with their poems. You could ask some children to write in riddle form, some to use alliteration, and others to try to use rhyme.

- Give children PCM 6 (page 23). Ask them to look for poems by some of the poets listed on the PCM, and fill in the PCM with the titles of the poems and a brief comment. Children (or you) could add the names of further poets to the list. This will also help children choose poems for class anthologies.

- Ask the children to use PCM 7 (page 24) to complete their own nonsense version of *The World of Weird*, adding their own words.

ASSESSMENT

At the end of the unit, you may want to take a little time to look in-depth at a piece of a child's writing that has been completed either independently or as part of a guided session. You may already have observed this during guided sessions. Teaching assistants can also observe children during shared sessions, assessing their abilities against the key objectives.

At the end of this Unit, you can assess the child's ability to meet the following statements and objectives.

The following chart covers the relevant NLS objectives for Year 2 Term 1. If using the shared and guided writing sessions suggested for other terms, you will find opportunities to cover a range of NLS objectives for Year 2 Term 2 and Year 2 Term 3. The relevant objectives are listed on page 5.

Sessions	NLS Objectives	NLS Target Statements for Writing
All sessions	T7 to learn, reread and recite favourite poems, taking account of punctuation; to comment on aspects such as word combinations, sound patterns and forms of presentation	<u>Consider and select from alternate word choices.</u> ● Are children able to identify powerful uses of language in poems they read, and apply these to their own writing? ● Can children identify some of the main features of different types of poems, such as rhyme, rhythm, alliteration etc., and use these in their own writing?
All sessions	T12 to use simple poetry structures and to substitute own ideas, write new lines	<u>Begin to show some characteristics of chosen form.</u> ● Are children able to write their own poems with some of the features and structure of poems they have read? <u>Write initial jottings, notes and ideas before writing.</u> ● Do children plan and write notes when starting a poem, particularly when the form or layout is relatively complex?

In all sessions, children should be practising correct handwriting, spelling and grammar.

Consolidation

If a child is struggling to reach one of these targets, you may need to revisit the problem area. For children who find poetry writing difficult, the best preparation is to read and enjoy more poetry, either alone, in a group or with adult support. You could support children by working with them on oral versions of poems they like, working their ideas up until they are confident enough to put them in writing. You could work together with a child as he or she tackles one of the PCMs, discussing the task in detail before the child writes.

Extension

If a child has successfully achieved these targets, you could ask them to read more poems from the two mini-anthologies. They could choose a favourite poem and write their own version. They could also tackle some of the other PCMs independently.

Blue

Blue is the colour

_____

Blue is the colour

_____

Blue is the colour

_____

Blue is the colour of

_____

Recipe for a _____

Ingredients:

The Seaside, the Seaside

The seaside, the seaside, sitting at the seaside

What better way to get away

Than sitting at the seaside!

The Washing Line

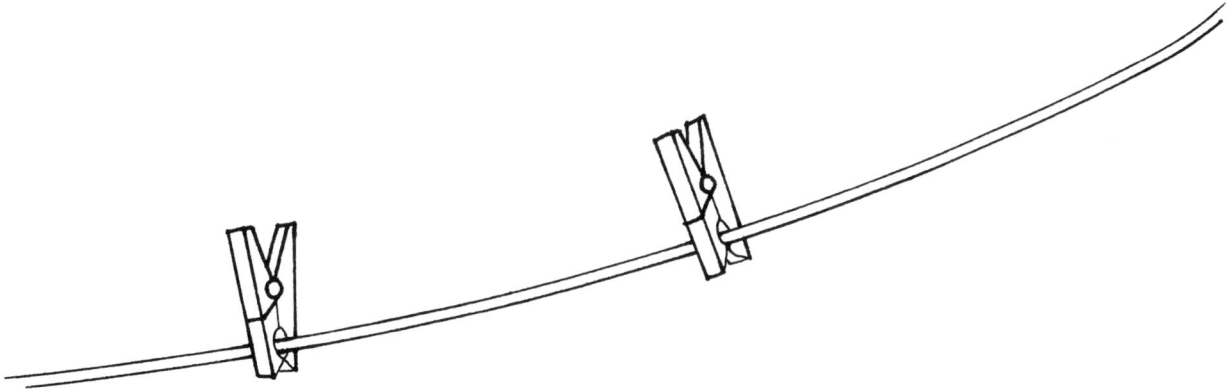

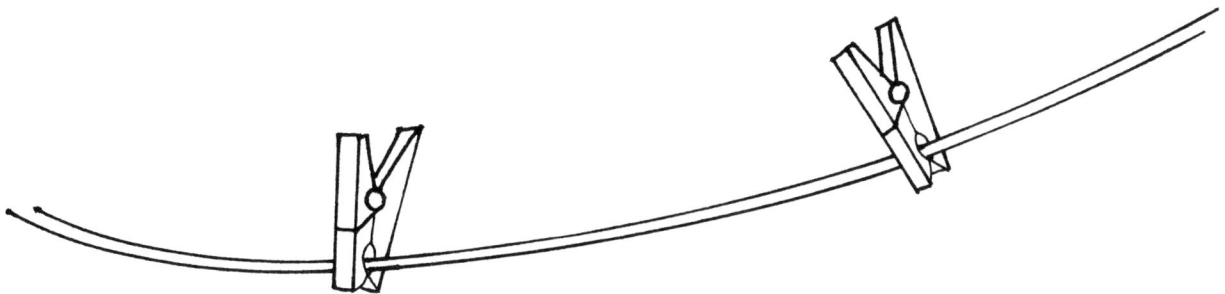

Snail Word Bank

Independent Writing

Poet	Title of Poem	Comment
Colin McNaughton		
John Foster		
John Agard		
Judith Nicholls		
Michael Rosen		
Robert Louis Stevenson		

My Weird World

In the world of Weird

All the _____ wear _____

And the _____ keep _____ in their _____,

The girls _____ _____ and live like _____

And the boys grow _____ on their _____.

In the world of Weird

All the _____ are _____

And the _____ are as _____ as can be,

_____ are _____, and grow in the _____

Or down at the bottom of the sea.